COMBUSTION

COMBUSTION

Lorri Neilsen Glenn

Brick Books

National Library of Canada Cataloguing in Publication

Neilsen Glenn, Lorri
    Combustion / Lorri Neilsen Glenn

Poems.

ISBN-13: 978-1-894078-55-9
ISBN-10: 1-894078-55-1

I. Title.

PS8577.E3373C64 2007 C811'.6   C2006-906537-3

We acknowledge the Canada Council for the Arts, the Government of
Canada through the Book Publishing Industry Development Program
(BPIDP), and the Ontario Arts Council for their support of our
publishing program.

Cover and author photographs by Allan Neilsen.

The book is set in Bembo and Rotis Serif.

Design and layout by Alan Siu.

Brick Books
431 Boler Road, Box 20081
London, Ontario N6K 4G6

www.brickbooks.ca

For my family

Contents

Brother   11

Smooth Rock from Lawrencetown Beach   12

Signal Hill, NL   13

Girl on the Sidewalk   14

Another Moon   15

Away (1)   17

Coming and Going   18

Labradorite   19

Daybreak   20

Appointment   25

Geranium   26

Fell   28

Strange Familiar   29

Annie Mae's Hands   30

Seven Threnodies for the Ordinary   31

A Young Bride Reads Canada's
   National Magazine   37

Combustion   42

Rebirth from a Snow House:
   Notes on Building a Quinsy   44

Lineage: On the Death of a Parent   46

Open   47

Winter Halls   48

Away (2)   49

Different   50

Good Fences   53

Saturday Night at the Shore Club   55

Crows in the Bedford Basin   59

Reading Charles Wright on a Rainy Morning   60

Birthday in Middle Age   61

Over for Dinner   62

The Rose and Thistle: Another Round   63

Grey   65

Phenomenology, Or Later, that Same Day...   69

Prosody: Some Advice   70

Not Far from Here   72

Hold   74

Notes   77

Acknowledgements   78

Biography   79

Brother

Our provenance: cold silence, lukewarm
creamed tuna on toast. Every movement
a mute apology. Five years' difference

means nothing; that we held our breath together
everything. This morning your step on the stairs
to the guest room so quiet I can hear the kitchen clock

four decades away. So quiet I can hear your clarinet
begin to call over the aspen and across the tracks,
and I get up, put on a fresh pot, crack eggs,

chop basil, find myself humming an old
Prine tune about angels and living,
about one thing to hold on to.

Smooth Rock from Lawrencetown Beach

Round and purple as a plum, accidental
kindness tossed from the rough

grip of the Atlantic. Teach me
concentration. Where darkness goes. How

time laughs. That memory,
like you, is shucked from mystery, rests

snug in my hand. The wind breathes
frost: listen! Blood,

singing.

Signal Hill, NL

You spy it next to your foot, glinting
under the wind-bitten scrub that clings
to the bank. Obsidian, you think, the word
itself a jewel, but no, more likely granite, custodian of this
bleak point where the wind's good arm can pitch you over the edge

with ease, alms for the Atlantic. The smooth stone in your fist
an unblinking optic of this land of ice and rock that breaks
death open in your fingers. And so you lean, an arc against the cold
wall of wind where Marconi drew
a line of sound, meridian of the human voice,

across the air and over water, before words became contagion,
before signals crackled skies, wilding like the sea itself. Granite sweetens
against your skin, picks up scattered tales. Like you: wandering unbuttoned
in your devil-dancing coat, looking into the eye of the sun as it cuts through
The Narrows, leaning forward, clutching a piece of the brink.

Girl on the Sidewalk

clatters a stick on the fence, this auditor of cement
cracks, fallen feathers. Above, implacable blue. The animated

geometry of her red coat, duck and dip, her hair
dendrites of white against November's wind. Leaves buck

above the tufts of grass shaled in ice, dried-blood scent
of summer gone. Porches squeeze themselves shut, gardens

have bartered their greenery for copper's tiny patience:
can they do this again? Eyes down, the girl walks

into these shoes: stick poised, grape-skin cheeks
bit by the sun, counting backward, counting ahead.

Another Moon

And yes, cirrus fingers across her eye. Old ink lake
                              of sky, hopeless

as desire. Skeins of snow unravel the road, city lights
                              behind & a room

an hour ahead. Road jockeys in Dodge Rams overtaking
                              every other mile,

radio voices falling away like dreams at dawn. Thirty below,
                              wind rocking your small

warm cell, and again it comes down to this:
                              You & a full moon

in the middle of the prairie. What else can you do but
                              drive, watch her light

catch the sway of a jet stream, swallow the bony lines
                              of the field, draw

hunger from the sheen of a silo sliding away in the night?
                              What names can you call her

she hasn't been called before? Sucker spawning moon,
                              moon when trees pop,

moon of the raccoon, little famine, chaste, snow. Why this
                              loyalty

to language? By the time a deer leaps from the corner of your eye

to the crossroad, flanks

lit, by the time you touch foot to brake, you want to erase an alphabet

of fifty years,

to offer up your name for her spare wisdom:

Moon. Lone. Winter.

Away (1)

*
It's always the same. You fashion
a nest of fruit, fur, familiar
songs.

*
Elms wait
along the road, concentrating
night into foliage.

*
Drunk on cold stars, you dip
a tin cup into the inkwell, spill
the river.

*
You find a whole morning in your pocket, stretch
it across your window. The wind
frantic with magpies.

*
To notice is to move.
Astonishment leaves tracks
pressed into words.

*
Just as the nest begins
to hum, you take it
apart, leave at dawn.

Coming and Going

Young voices like thrushes from the wiry trees
by the tracks. Toboggans, snowboards, swagger

and torque. It's Saturday. By the Co-op, her jaw snaps
gum, wind strums her hair as she waves, climbs

into the truck, leans into him as he puts it to the metal.
Outside the store, a huddle of eyes in parkas, possibility

in smoke rings. Sun setting, eros rising, you look
for shoes and a few bucks for a rye and coke, make

a list of what is leaving: an all-nighter, a ten-K, hanging
from Yamnuska, sailing to Panama, your feet sliding

on the scree of a day, what balance cares to learn
from risk. The mirror: cold window where you pass

yourself coming and going, where years, those frail birds,
carry spring in their throats while snow slips from the field.

Labradorite

The rest of my life is right here. Opens the box, grey rocks the size of a
woman's hand. Haven't seen this, I say. *Guy in Labrador ships it to me. A
wonder, this rock.* The texture of the coastline from the plane—ragged,
sharp, banking off the sea. Blunted. The sun is tentative outside the shop
window, wants to crawl inside. Tools on his workbench waiting, placid.
Look now. He has sprayed a piece with water, holds it under the light
clamped between us. Blue, silver, violet, green moving in sheets, and I
hold my breath under the smooth blade of his voice. *The Northern Lights
in there. That's where I'm going.* Meditative to work with, I say; and healing,
too, I'll bet. *That it is. Lord knows I can* —You know I still have some of
her things, I say. He looks up, polishing, curves a slow smile. Last time I
was here, I bought two Celtic pieces from her, and every time I look in
the drawer—*My sister had that effect. A lot of people say she isn't gone.* He
closes his eyes, rubs the surface of rock, this cleft in the earth, this cold,
dark source. The flat face of the mineral turns under the light, ray inside
refracting back and forth in layers below and below and below. *A kind of
feldspar,* he says. The light ricocheting, hues echoing, different wavelengths
coming and going. *See? Depends on the angle. You never know what you'll
find in here—flashes of silver, pink. You can get lost for hours.*

Daybreak

Sun on its knees in the field rinsed by dawn, splashed
in prayer. I walk

alone below the abbey, shoes sussing a way into sage
and a psalm

of the particular. Shadow climbs a hay bale ahead,
feet tripping

an exclamation of grasshoppers, the shutter of time.
Behind me,

a girl chews a stalk of wheat, lays her quivering tongue
on the saltlick,

ravishes the whiskered ground.
                                    Above, clouds

blooming. Dust, like the future, rises around her.
Cumulus

petals, path of a hawk, flange of foxtail, crusted blood
on her knee,

the sure and swarming horizon. The prairie teaching her
how to pay

attention. The heart is a hymnal, she does not know this
now, does not

hear the susurration beyond the hill, wind gathering
grief, gathering

yearning, shuddering nights, the cold eye
of the morning star.

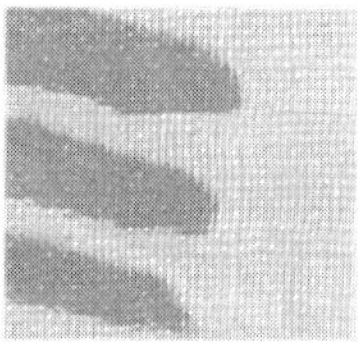

Appointment

Look, you tell yourself. Go there. Feel how her arms hug the depleted
belly, her eyes held steady on the infant tucked inside a carriage complicated

with two sets of wheels & gears & cute cotton print covers, hand-knit
wraps, a knotted bag of baby paraphernalia swinging above

the worn brown carpet as the door opens, closes, opens, blows spring
air against our feet. Notice her hair, dull, flattened & the sweat

pants stretched, it seems, from night into day, her grey gaze a contract.
Listen to the voice across the room: —*he's over 230, won't take those pills, won't*

check his blood sugar, always into the damned sweets—pick up Hall & Oates
in the background, shrill, giddy voice of an announcer. Look again:

find her unblinking, immobile as the deer you saw on the road
that spring, as your cat, eyes skyward, giving suckle to another undulation

of fur. Go there. Back to when you were a body with no choice, to days
of numb & dawning shock the horizon has folded in, its silver line

closing around you both, an embrace so secure you wonder
if you will breathe alone again.

Geranium

Face down in the flowerbed this time, whimpering. The others on the bench outside, their permed white curls blinking in the prairie wind, mouths hash marks of disdain. I leave the car running & Carolyn lifts her into the back seat. A red geranium petal crushed into her temple & those maroon polyester pants of hers with the elasticized waist drooped around a dark stain. God, I hate the smell of geraniums. Sad, sour, reactionary plants. Smug even. *He's been watching me.* She is trying to sit up now, growling. *Hand me that— you don't smoke. Give me one. What are you doing?* Her eyes in the rear-view mirror—forty years & they still feel like a slap. *He parks below my window, away from the entrance. That's stalking, you know. He's a nutcase. And no cheques. I have to take him to court again. Not. A. Dime.* I toss the butt out the window; it's made me dizzy. Carolyn & I will have to call the guys, tell them to feed the kids. Left my scotch on the table when the superintendent called. God, I probably smell just like her. Missed the turn—okay, around the block again. Carolyn is looking at me: say something. I know—we should say something. *Thirty-eight years, for what? Not a dime. Where the hell are you taking me?* Her face thrust between the front seats, dirt in her hair. I signal to turn & my hand shakes. My sister frowns at me, looks at her. You need some help, Carolyn starts. *I don't need your help, Missy. You haven't called for months. I don't need anyone's fucking help. I raised you girls, and you turned out just like him. How the hell, I don't know. Help!* Air rush. The back window rolling down. The door handle: *Help—Over here!* A kid with a skateboard outside the 7-Eleven looks over, then away. The light changes & I move into the intersection. Gravel sound from the open back door, as Carolyn crawls over the gearbox, a car behind me honking. *Just like him. The both of you. Oh, god. I'm so alone.* The maroon pants, her sensible shoes, sagging white belly, the curb. Brakes. City heat baked into the concrete. Lifting her from the street. Her arms swinging. My hair in her fist. Blood on her chin. My arm wet. A fire truck howling around the corner. Across the street, at the detox centre, a planter of treated wood & stems of bobbing red. Of course. Carolyn's eyes on me now: And you wonder, she says. You wonder.

Fell

Today we cut the tree. The wind's steel teeth
trolling the coast, squirrels pulsing

with seasonal radar: hurricane warning. Ready
to collapse on the roof, that pine

was, the heft of its blistered bark threatening
the eaves. Sometimes it comes to that:

tree or house. Tumour or Uncle Martin. Now
your chimney will draw, the man says; you have

more sky. Corks for god's wine bottles, tumbling
erratics, strewn behind the house like

an argument that fell apart on your tongue.
Squirrels will learn another route, who knows what

the hillside will remember: the canted craning
of an old grove, an arm

poised, sundering racket, the foil of a blade
draining warmth, shivering in the light.

Strange Familiar

To make the strange familiar. To take your notebook and recorder to fields
unknown to you, be participant observer, just as Margaret was, though

this pale and angular woman wrapped awkwardly in the embrace
of a bright sarong heard from gleeful village girls only what they knew

she wanted them to say. All invention—all once upon a time, these tales
of the field. Did you know the sixth sense of the observed sent signals

from above the tree-line to below the Amazon? That when you gazed
upon informants gazing back at you, another text was being written:

write what you wish, white jester. Later you will dance in our stories
wearing that odd hat, those clumsy shoes. Burnt nose twitching

over your tight mouth. Your blind blue eyes. You thought civilization
began and ended with a pen, a bible, table linen, a queen, the precision

of a motor, a queue at the station. Where was the ethnographer
recording you, documenting your wanton appetite for whatever's

in your path, because all the world is your dominion, because
all of it is food?

Annie Mae's Hands

I intend to be one of those raggedy-ass Indians, she told them, a grizzly
bear mother, a warrior working the combat zone, savage with a pure

heart. It took five to dig the grave, bury the body, a bullet in the head, hands
missing, shipped somewhere across the country as evidence. Annie

was a threat. Wilma Blacksmith dropped her shovel, lay in the dirt to measure:
We might as well learn to bury each other. One more silent mouth scooped

out of Wallace Little's ranch. Later, the winds—yellow, black, white
and red—howling cold, howling murder. On the bier, tobacco, moccasins,

beaded clothes for Annie to take beyond. What once grasped babies'
fingers, traced men's bodies, picked berries, held guns, waved

signs in Boston fell in the dust on a Pine Ridge battlefield of two. Imagine
the knife, bite of that winter day, waxy stain of blood, how he walked

away with her hands, unaware that they reach from the other
side of silence, then and now, ribboning the wind, signing.

Seven Threnodies for the Ordinary

One: Boys

Only six in our graduation and they
all went over—four
didn't come back. Four from one
small Manitoba farming
town. This: Donald Beamish
in his uniform.
I would have married him.

Two: Cat

You saw a flash, heard
a thump. Drove on, didn't
look back. Later, you mourn:
how you will never know
a name, a story,
whether you could ask,
be forgiven.

Three: Faith

After the axes and the crowbars, we haul
it all to the dump: pews, apse, good wood,
stained glass. I was ten when
he told me to touch him, felt
something wet. Others, younger. No one
speaks. We stand under the Northern
lights, set the fire.

Four: Progress

Another waterfront hole for the high
life rising to claim the horizon
through fog: gulls swarm around wrappers,
butts, Tim's empty cups, spools of coiled
wire, and buckets that ransack the ground, toss
loam and roots
as cement churns, stiffening.

Five: A Jar from the Margaree

Bare-footed and blind, he drops
the fruit jar on the kitchen floor:
a thousand pieces. The next morning,
the carpet dotted with dark tracks
like birds writing on snow. Had that jar
in this house for fifty years, he said:
that's how everything goes.

Six: Budding

The man leaves her in the bushes afterward;
she walks five miles home. Her father
shows her the door; she has damaged the Lord's
goods. Today, by the bus stop, she holds
the brown-eyed bundle. Faith
is growing something,
wholly new.

Seven: White Birch

Always behind the screen
of your consciousness, calling. Sense began there,
beside the papered trunk where being turned
to knowing. You see it in a photograph
years later, and the lock of recognition
tumbles open, each spring-driven branch clicking
body into place.

A Young Bride Reads Canada's National Magazine

November, 1921: Ethel Glenn, expectant mother, sits with her tea to read the latest edition of *Maclean's*, brought from the post office by her husband, Bill, on his way to the hockey rink where he was a well-known figure on the ice.

20 Cents. $3.00 a year. Volume XXXIV. Number Nineteen. Contents: The Pebble, by M.L.C. Pickthall, illustrated by Dudley G. Summers. Will Canada Go Yellow? Part II, Union Labor at the Cross-roads. Women and their Work, with two features: There's Amazing Food Value in Dried Fruits and Getting Seven Children Off to a Good Start.

Seven. Ethel is carrying her first child, whom they will name Grace, after Ethel's younger sister who fell through a hole in the ice while skating and whom Ethel and her brothers almost saved, grabbed Grace's scarf but felt it slip away. Ethel comes from a family of thirteen children. Who knows what lies ahead?

This is a true story…seven young Hodgins, very creditable specimens of the four-square development standard—father a master printer of outstanding ability…salary of thirteen dollars and twenty-five cents a week…mother a former teacher…Mr. Hodgins a fanatic on the question of home-buying…

Bill and Ethel are thinking about building, cannot stay on the brother's farm much longer.

Ethel pauses, re-reads what Hodgins says: *Years ago when electric wiring was a new thing a bride would see the lights and say "oh yes, John, let's take this house, it's wired." And what else could he do? A little later when builders began putting in cheap mantels the mantel would sell the house. The next fad was building cement wash-tubs in the basement: a woman liked to tell her friends that she had 'stationary tubs'.*

Enough of that, Ethel thinks. Turns to the section, *Maybe Adam Laughed at These*, for something lighter:

The train drew up with a mighty crash and shock between stations. "Is it an accident?" inquired a worried-looking individual of the conductor. "Some one pulled the bell cord!" shouted the conductor. "The express knocked our last car off the track! Take us four hours before the track is clear!" "Great Scott! Four hours! Why, man, I am to be married today!" groaned the passenger. The conductor, a bigoted bachelor, raised his eyebrows suspiciously. "Look here," he demanded. "I suppose you ain't the chap that pulled the cord?"

Smiles. Her father is a CPR rail engineer out of Schreiber, the small Ontario town where Ethel herself will be buried sixty-three years from now. This she does not know, of course. Nor does she know that in six years, 1927, friends and relatives will gather for her father's funeral, his death the result of a landslide on the track near Fire Hill.

Ah, here is a pen sketch of a family, the mother seated holding a jewelry box. The name *Elgin: Faithful Guardian of Time* in large letters below. The caption: "Oh, children! For me! But it's—it's lovely for a girl of twenty." *Hitherto mother's gifts had been purely practical— middle-aged. But this birthday was different.* "I'd love to be young again, just to have a wrist-watch," *mother had chanced to say one day. She had forgotten, but her children had remembered.*

Drowsy now. Where will Ethel spend her middle years? Will her children bring her presents? Too soon Ethel will be widowed, as her mother was. She will move from the small town of Shoal Lake into Winnipeg to work as a nurse in the General and live with her sister Gertrude, also a widow, in a compact, doily-upholstered house near Corydon, a house her granddaughter will love for the imposing dark brown radio with the brown mesh voicebox, and Ethel's faded cloth-covered hope chest filled with pillow cases embroidered with pink and yellow roses.

A headline in the Review of Reviews section stops her: *No Peace While U.S. Arms: Japan Convinced She is to be Forced into New War.* Three of Ethel's brothers didn't come home in 1918, and she wonders about Bill, her husband, and about any sons she might bear. Flips past the Quaker Oats Company advertisements for Puffed Wheat and Puffed Rice, Baker's Cocoa, Curzon Brothers Limited: *English Suits from $22.50 delivered to any address in Canada with customs and all other charges paid.* She doesn't have $22.50. Now this looks interesting: *golden-hued Pyrex takes the place of pot and pan drudgery.* Ethel left the beef bone on the stove before she came to bed. Perhaps Bill will put it in the shed when he hangs up his skates, lays his woolen jersey by the fire. *Ivory Soap*, she reads: *the charm of fine underthings depends as much upon the suggestion of sweet immaculate cleanliness as upon exquisite texture and painstaking needlework—every woman of refinement will acknowledge this.*

Too late to heat water now, fill up the tub in the kitchen and bathe before Bill comes home. Pillar of the community, Bill is, and his unborn daughter Grace will tell her own grandchildren years later about his talents as a violinist and a hockey player, how her father met her mother in Kelloe when Ethel nursed a family through the flu of 1918, will tell how, suddenly, Bill's life would end on Valentine's

Day night when Ethel was working the night shift at the Shoal Lake hospital, and thirty-nine-year-old William Glenn, as he was called in the Shoal Lake paper, *"felt out of condition and left the ice, made his way to the barber shop and secured a bottle of cream soda to give him relief. While in the act of drinking this he slumped and the boys thought he had fainted. He was laid on one of the tables and the doctor called immediately who upon arrival pronounced life to be extinct. Word was taken to his sister, Mrs. Laura Shomperlen. This, although tactfully given, proved to be disastrous. Mrs. Shomperlen had not been feeling well and this sad news proved to be the breaking point as she in turn swooned and never regained consciousness, lying in a state of coma for fifty-five hours, finally passing away on Saturday morning at 5 o'clock."*

The Shoal Lake paper does not say they emptied William John Glenn's pocket before placing the body in the icehouse by the cemetery to await burial in the spring, does not say they found a Valentine card addressed to his nine-year-old daughter, Grace, who waited at home for him.

Ethel glances at her hope chest, tucked under the window, where she once kept her lace undergarments. The lid of this hope chest will become a table top in her granddaughter's cottage in the Maritimes but Ethel, of course, is thinking not of the next century, but of the small life quickening inside her. Of Grace. Of rising early in the cold to walk to the end of the road for a ride to work the next morning. Of Bill, who will be coming in the door any moment, sweaty, that relaxed, spent look in his eyes. Decides to pretend to be asleep tonight; in fact, she may well be—she's that weary. Work, then the doctor's, then the hot work of boiling and canning chickens.

She reaches to turn down the lamp, but the drawing for the first story, *The Pebble*, catches Ethel's eye. *Bernard considered her,* the caption read. *He saw that she could not believe him, though she was longing to be able to.* A ramshackle wooden house; a lopsided picket fence, a young woman in a loose dress, holding a summer hat, standing with a man at a crossroad—could be anywhere in small-town Canada. And it looks to be a love story. Yes, that will do. Begins: *Maybe something like this happened. Two angels leaned on the wall of heaven, looking down on the Clearwater country. They were strong angels. One seemed especially capable and quick on the wing. He had need to be.*

Combustion

And so the nuns put my little brother Jack into the furnace, and that was that. My mother doesn't know until she wakes, the white shoes a whisper by her bed, my father's voice cold sand in her ear. And I, at home, curled near the heat register, Gram despairing that I won't eat. Won't eat. Waiting for the baby. Snowball sits on the back of the chesterfield, watching what wind does in the claws of bare trees, drifts outside too high and wilding for her paws, too high for me and my snowsuit. Too high, too cold. And the black phone on the wall. And no baby. Fine then, no soup. *They decided*, she says now, fifty years away, as we sit on the deck, our skin inhaling summer-waning sun. *The holy Trinity. Doctor, nun, husband. Dead of winter. They could have waited until I saw my son's face.* She stuffs out her cigarette, rolls her head back. That distance—where she goes. I reach, grasp only the howl of storms in the small railway town, fist of cold at the door in winter, maw of Main Street under high clouds and summer dust. My father's voice at supper—*they fired the stationmaster today:* image of a man tied to a pole over a bonfire. The July parade: crepe paper, my white peaked hat and apron, the Old Dutch Cleanser woman. Joey, hobbling beside me, brown-fringed hat and holster. The water tower the highest thing in the world at the end of the road. Drums. And the Switzer girls on their tricycles ahead of us, gone the next winter. Fire, their whole house down. Clang of the coal stove, my father shovelling at dawn. Heat. Cold. Mother. Gram. Cat. And the empty space where a baby was going to be. I could pull out the old Brownie photos, crisp and snapping from their little crow-wing tabs, burn those into my mind. But how to go back on my own. To go where she goes, even to the edge. She pulls out her lighter again. The DuMaurier, a small white finger in her mouth, sparks. Ash. *Lying there, cut from my gut to my ribs. Sick from ether. Out cold. And he comes home from Hinton in time to tell them to go ahead. Dispose of the body. Small town. Small hospital. And you at home, waiting.* Stillborn. A brother. Out the chimney into the air, the whole town breathing him. Her smoke drifts off the deck toward the trees, white mark in the air, a wavering trail.

Rebirth from a Snow House:
Notes on Building a Quinsy

1.

Pile high and wait. Trust in the physics of snowflakes, strength
of the waning moon. Leave gossip to the magpie. Empty
the centre, one white scoop
at a time. Prepare a dream for the interior.

2.

Crawl in, fingers at the precipice, back through the tunnel
that emptied you on November's frozen floor,
into Margaret's hands as she hangs the crystalline
man-shapes on her Monday morning line,
into Bill's shoulder as he scrapes a hand-carved stick across
the Strathclair rink, past the river's rupture
where only Grace's scarf was found until run-off
in the spring, then dig northward where Couture from Paris
sent a son to meet his country wife, a Great Plains Cree. To the east,
your hands cold compass needles, your ears
membranes of a distal ocean recalling Manannan mac Lir,
trickster in the mists, or Finn MacCool perhaps,
his foolish games with hazel sticks.
Burrow.

3.

Until you find the quickening
spark, blessed spool that sprung
from who knows where or what, unravelling
down the centuries, then:
try to grasp it, turn around.

4.

Emerge from some lacuna, dusted
white, delivered into wings of the familiar. Gather thunder
into a cry, grey sky eyeing it all through wet
lashes of trees: these trees, the ones bending
now to cover you, you've come so far, old meadow
grass glistening like dry fish in your mouth.

Lineage: On the Death of a Parent

Carry the letter into the future, words burning
with grace only you can read. Blue winter light
translates your reflection at the water's edge: eyes

salted with secrets. Your hand the last signature.
Grief is the forest you enter, confused
by the doxa of ritual around you, path radiant

with ruin. Smoldering on the margin.
The clearing where meaning is the residue
of time. The perfection of the ash.

Open

Your room unlocked those summer days
by the river. Cash, keys, a bottle of gin, loose silk
shirts, a watch, a well-thumbed collection
of short stories—all abandoned
like spilled spoons on the floor of a dream.

Wind in the afternoon lifting
the curtains, sails of ships,
Marilyn Monroe's white dress unfurling above
the subway vent, lives you wanted
to live, your lungs: everything

that fills, empties, fills again.
Sun in your eyes a pearl pried from a dark shell,
glinting inside your bones. And you,
the river, all the wet
hollows of the earth, opening.

Winter Halls

Outside the window, exhaust fog, blue morning over the Red River
valley stretching wide on the jangled days of late December. White

fingers over light-streaming cars, fan belts screaming in the boulevard
rush. *CJOB News. 31 below.* Down the hall the elevator catches,

whines. Odours of buttered toast and coffee thread the corridors
where the burn of deep sleep dissipates, where dreams lose shape

like breath coming in from the street. A *Free Press* by one door. Tinsel
taped on another. A stocking the size of a child's empty coat splays red

and white on Number 1430. A spoon falls, chitters behind a wall. Below
a phone: two rings. A cough. At the end of the hall a violin trying, trying

to fly, sound dipping like wings in a gale, groping for the old
tunes. Add the years here: ten thousand, more, marked in grey hair and

bunions. Five hundred grandchildren, iterations of seasoned bodies
circumnavigating the globe as these hallways begin to stir. More stories

here than hands of rummy, than caches of saved string and twist
ties, tucked into cupboards; tales knowing their place, like the

well-dusted Hummel child, turned just so, firing light into memory, rosy
cheeks bright and fierce as the tiny black shoes tied with a bow.

Away (2)

Sew yourself inside retreat while
the air sweeps away city clutter

with the dedication of an old peasant
in a folk tale you remember only for the heft

of the woman. Her misguided industry.
The broom. Wonder about the marks

under your skin: years of names, rhythms,
signs. You are here, inside

the plump weave of trees whose barbs spring
through dark's ticking and the sea rinses

the long day lightly, loosely on the rocks.
You think *spruce*. You think *tide*.

A bird splays its wings: You see crucifixion.
Where can you go to reach for the invisible?

The open needle, intangible thread.
The empty eye.

Different

As I watch you turtle-
backed go down the hill

to catch the bus I wish
you had a Joey in your

life to go with you, Joey who
walked beside me, brown

foot-high shoe a magnet
for the laughter he ignored,

or rheumy Jean who was so
kind but never used a tissue,

left trails of snot and tears
on all our memories of Grade

Four. Or good old Hubert,
dozy smile and slow

illumination as we plotted
by the woodshed, mashing

bugs and carving towns
from dirt. So simple they

all were, the days I mean,
when everyone was just

a stripe crossed with others
in a busy plaid, a nut

tossed in with bolts
and nails, a dandelion among

the Queen Anne's lace
and quack grass by the schoolyard

fence, when summers were
still feral and small worlds

forgave us all for being, just
for being. You once fit

in my cupped hands, lay
in the blanket box

for months beside our
bed where we could

hear your tinny cry,
and you could feed

on our imagination:
will you walk, or talk, will

you learn to read, can
you prove the doctors

wrong, and when will
all the eyes and tongues

begin to carve the scars
behind your skin? What

shoes can we make for
your path now, what hand-

kerchief will dry the sea
that rises higher at your door?

Good Fences

"Everyone all right over there?" The neighbour on the phone like she's asking, "anyone for a beer?" or "How're those tomatoes doin'?" and me, holding the receiver, hearing again the thump, feeling myself jump from the bed to see him on the bathroom floor, mumbling nonsense, to see his eyes trying to fight the undertow, and then I have the phone in hand, the same one I am holding now, but that night it is shaking and I hear the first birds stirring, and the dispatcher on the other end is patient: "Is he breathing? Is he conscious?" and I am pulling words from my throat like hair from a brush, tangled, thin, then the fireman, his young son, their vehicle in the driveway, and the ambulance, and my husband, grey as the end of winter, wheeled away into god knows what's going to happen next. Again, she's saying "Everyone okay?" and my words are on a leash, taut, tugging hard at my chest: you know goddamn well things are not all right. I saw your lights on through the trees when they slid him through the big white doors of that vehicle and it's two days later so you're not calling because you're concerned; you're calling because you're nosy, you're calling because Wanda from down the hill brought her brood up to your house this morning, I saw them pass our driveway, and the two of you have been drinking coffee and talking, and this is just your bald curiosity—you don't even have the decency to name it as such. Everyone all right? Well, fuck you. But I take a deep breath, force a smile into my voice, say, "He's fine now. It was a scare, I'll tell you that. It was a scare." What the scare was you'll never know, sweetheart, because I won't give you that. Like I've kept the extra change when I've paid too much already, given her the plonk and left the good bottle in the cupboard. And now, her voice: "Wanda was wondering too, you know. First thing she asked this morning—'do you know what happened over there,' she says, 'because I got up when I heard the siren, got dressed, came halfway up the driveway,' she says, Wanda's thinking it might be us, or the baby, but when she saw it wasn't, that it was at your house, not ours, she went back to bed." "Oh," I said, holding the phone like a freshly dead mouse. "Oh," I said. And: "Well, how about you? How's your growing family?"

Saturday Night at the Shore Club

Wanna dance? Cocks his head, swigs. Stumbles up from the folding chair, grabs her hand, swims into the light and the bobbing mass under the fishnet ceiling. From the back door, puffs of cool wet air, the sleeve of an August night, stuttering of headlights up from the cove. It's two drinks past awareness on a Saturday night and The Prime Minister of the Blues and his boys punch a beat across the wooden floor. Sweet feast of odours: fried onions, salty burgers, popcorn, drift of coconut oil, someone's spray of Charlie, another's Brut. Shards of colour: burnished shoulders, pink cotton, faded denim, green parrot shirts, spaghetti strap T's. Sheen of the old wood walls. Sweat-soaked bodies rocking, small cup of escape. Stories began here, are beginning now. You've been here for two hours or twenty years. *The Maritimes' oldest dance hall.* Grandson of the founder gathers bottles from tables by the stone fireplace, carries in his genes the 200-year-old memory of a sea battle and a large copper pot from the Chesapeake. Tender faces with beards, mascara, crow's feet—when did this happen?—emerging from the line at the bar, laughter rising. Along the back, watchers, reluctant dancers, newly-arrived from the cabins and from the city, lined up, mouths open. You couldn't hear if you wanted to, and that's okay. It's the pulse, the staccato steps, hips, bumps and desire, whoops when Dutchie digs deep into the downbeat of "Blue Suede Shoes," limbs fuelled by last fires. You are nineteen, you are sixty-five, eyes caught by the spotlight where the drummer's shirt sticks to his chest, guitars flash and roar—*you can burn my house, steal my car*—near closing time, a slow dance, glass bottles rattled into boxes, the scrape of abandoned chairs. Last call. After this beer, this dance, this rum-soaked proposition, Saturday night's possibilities turn a corner. Music stops; lights go on. Down the path to the beach, what's left of a summer moon cuts a groove through the trees, reckless light falling on driftwood and sand.

Crows in the Bedford Basin

come as the sun
goes. Dead Sisters
of Charity, they say, returning
to the motherhouse on the hill to perch
on November's thin branches. Along the shore
below, a train speaks
an iron sentence around the harbour, shivering
                             houses with its call:

blood comes home
in the dark, light comes
home in the dark.

Reading Charles Wright on a Rainy Morning

As souls slip through the arms
of the trees, puddle in the tired
grass. Do not despair: their blue
light will course through earth's small
arteries. After time, we are still
moving. The garbage truck roars, a man
in a slicker swings fat bags stuffed with leaves up
and away. Underground or above, we are all
changing places. But now, now we remain, returning
to Sunday, always Sunday: the only word
that sounds like beginning.

Birthday in Middle Age

At the window, you see the harbour chop
in gestures of abandonment. Someone says: consider
the alternative. And: enjoy, you won't get
out of this alive. Your aging mother's
yearly chime: *Tromping through the snow, water*
broken, the hospital two blocks away and your aunt
running behind, flapping: you'll catch your death!

So, each lacy card a shovel. Sun shudders time
in the red of your raised glass: ribbons cut,
wrapping crumpled into peaks of hollow
mountains, tender membranes:
before. After.

Over for Dinner

Inside, *Strangelove* flickers black and white, the cold
hole of its philosophy gives you vertigo, and Sellers'

angular face, a dialogue of chiaroscuro, promises
nothing. So you leave the others, their rueful laughter,

eyes dimmed with drink, and look for her outside. This
darkening shape in the October air is how winter

comes. Must be half a pack she's gone through, you
pull on one, the smoke sand in your lungs. Vertigo,

again. I don't see the point, she says. Of anything.
You ask: what do you want to leave, how will

we remember you? Aren't you meant for
something? She inhales, shakes her head: one

foot after another, she says. Only for him: I couldn't
do that to him. Wind gone, stars blaze behind the pines,

the valley a dark cave and clouds funnelling
into the white hole in the centre of night. Silence

sits between you, holding everything, holding nothing at all.

The Rose and Thistle: Another Round

Anyway, my eyes are not accustomed to this light…
Lew DeWitt, "Flowers on the Wall"

The heat outside is mango and cabana, but this is St. John's. The
harbour still holding a handful of summer inside its cape. Lights dot
The Narrows on your way down from the hill. It's almost eleven, and
the music won't start for a while yet, but you want to do this: you
want to trade sleep for Lady Luck and the Smoking Guns. To be
with friends, other loners and watchers, maybe to talk, let yourself be
taken over by the night. Be infected with a beat, laugh at Stan's wit, a
wit so dry you want to feed it, bottle by bottle, until you see it
coming. You want to wake up in the morning feeling more at home
in this harbour. Ah, your head: too cramped for this large, generous
night. Music, you think—music will drive your self-absorption out
the door, past Water Street, past The Brow. Here's Michael, his grin,
and a heft of Jack Daniels. Across from you a guy whoops at random,
his own soundtrack. Someone lies the length of the bench, sings
along to Johnny Cash. A hulk of a man two feet from the tiny stage
runs his hands in buddy's hair. Two women erupt at an opening
chord, stuff their cigarettes in ashtrays, bop onto the floor. One is a
mover, skin peeking through a stretched turquoise tank, the other, in
black, reminds you of a bear. You are smoking by default, and it is
seductive. God how you miss those nights of cigarettes and two and a
juice, another round, and another, nights you fell into because you
knew, when sunlight sliced the wall the next morning, it opened up
everything you could be, and so much was still there. *I'm so fuckin'*—
but you can't hear the rest of what the guy says, you only see his

head fall on the table. You and your friends laugh, you have front row seats to this dance, to the band, to tomorrow's stories. The girl singer holds the mic like a bouquet, or a child's face, and the drummer tucked next to the door beats on the only drums he could find. This is tonight for you. All there is. Pay attention. The nights are longer from here on in.

Grey

Red did time in juvie, sucked on his first smoke at eight. Blue trails
behind St. Jude, wringing her hands, simpering. Green tries too
                                                    damned hard.
Yellow, that slut, loves everything with a pulse, vacuums naked, rubs
citrus on her skin. And orange? Neurotic, high octane: ten pages
in the DSM. Keep him from guns, fat-tire trucks, fuses.

Go, instead, with grey: hum of an engine you trust. An A-
chord—major, minor, seventh. Placid as a cat and sly
about small spaces, quiet at the gates of language. Stone
path to the Buddha you killed. A single shoe
at the bottom of the lake. Old man's beard
in your apple tree, the alchemy of light
into lattice, draping over dead limbs. Bruise

of a frail wind. The achromatopic among you see
tone, shadow, saturation: the grain
but not the rainbow. Why call this blindness?
You trust moonlight, love
the evening before, the morning after. Grey is your true
love's hair, your favourite sweater with the fraying sleeve,
grandmother's tarnished silver passed hand to hand. Sand in the oyster
shell. Necklace of whispers
sliding down your breast.

Phenomenology, Or Later, that Same Day...

The cat comes back, the doctor calls,
things happen in ways you can only
begin to imagine. The story
comes after, remember? You turn
the strange into familiar with what is
at hand. Most of your life is like this:
memory, mercy, the ballast
of desire, heavier for the words
you've wrapped around them,
and lighter too.

Prosody: Some Advice

1.
Sing the cave
in twenty-six notes
for twice that many years.

2.
It's dark inside, lub-dub,
lub-dub, and your ribs
have dancing shoes.

3.
Coil a rope
above your head, like this.
Twirl the circle, twirl and aim.

4.
Or watch the water becoming
still. Fall in without
a ripple.

5.
Stir with a spoon, but
don't infer the stone
from the soup.

6.
Lay yourself on
a dry page, soak
under the sun.

7.
Until.

Not Far from Here

You open the door to a small town inside:
yolk-yellow mornings, a freckle-faced

paper boy and his rifle arm: nasturtiums
again. Labour that pauses—hold that—

at the noon whistle for homemade soup
ladled by the one who hangs your summer

clothes breathing Sunlight Soap, reaches high
on the back stoop—nice morning, Betty!—

to pin the wooden beak just where shoulder
meets sleeve. A wave to the milkman rattling

past in his empty truck as you wade into the heat-
soaked afternoon to the Chinese café, a quarter

in your damp hand for fries and gravy, a dime
for cream soda kept in the cooler, pulled up

like a pickerel shaking off water, up like hope,
wet and icy as wonder. And now hear

evening's engines burn along Main
Street, trace the thread of voices knotted

in the kitchen, pot roast again, your sister's
turn to dry. Watch silver stitches outside

the wooden window sash begin to blink—of course
they blink—as you slip under the rustle

of down, as the lens dollies out: long shot
of chimneys and rooftops, fat moon, distant

rails and plume, soundtrack swelling over
the steel-sweeping soft-shoe of lonesome

boxcars rolling, rolling. MCMLVII.

Hold

Worlds turn

on this: sorrow sees itself
in the mirror, and, behind,
the shadow of joy. Your world lies

on the bed, emaciated
limbs curled into an old sea,
lips so dry you can no longer

moisten them with your own. The nurse says
"it's time to gather
around," and the room

empties of what you knew
all along had no name. You see
them spinning in the light: love,

loss, love, loss, love,
loss. Turn. At the door:
seasons

reach for your hands: hold.

Notes

"Annie Mae's Hands". The body of Anna Mae Pictou Aquash was found in 1976; FBI investigators cut off her hands. A M'ikm'aq born in Nova Scotia in 1945, Annie Mae was active in the American Indian Movement. Arlo Looking Cloud was convicted of her murder in 2004; the conviction is being appealed.

The text used in "A Young Bride Reads Canada's National Magazine" is taken from a print copy of the November, 1921 edition of *Maclean's*, Volume 34 (19), and from the *Shoal Lake Star*.

"Rebirth from a Snow House: Notes on Building a Quinsy". Information about Manannan mac Lir and Finn MacCool from *A Dictionary of World Mythology* by Arthur Cotterell. Oxford: Oxford University Press, 1997 (pg. 168 and 158) ISBN 0-19-217747-8

Acknowledgements

Several of these poems have been published in an earlier form in the following journals, books, anthologies, and online publications, *Grain, Arc, Contemporary Verse 2, Prairie Fire, Not Just Any Dress, Third Floor Lounge, CBC Radio Three, Literacy and Living, The Society, Nth Position, White Ink, Saved String,* and *Dance the Guns to Silence: 100 Poems for Ken Saro-Wiwa.* My thanks to the editors and judges.

"Brother" is for Brian Boggs. "Lineage" is for Don McKay. "Different" is for Jesse Neilsen. "Daybreak" is for Jan Zwicky. "The Rose and Thistle: Another Round" is a response to Stan Dragland's *12 Bars.* "Rebirth from a Snowhouse" is for David Carpenter, Honor Kever, and Dave Margoshes. My thanks to Catherine Martin for information about Anna Mae Pictou Aquash.

Sincere thanks to members of In the Field, the contemplative philosophy group of 2004-2006; to members and faculty of the Banff Writing Studio 2004 and to the Nova Scotia Division of Tourism, Culture and Heritage; to Kathy, Carole, Eleonore, and Matilka; to the women who've inspired these poems, including my mother and grandmothers; to a chorus of necessary friends; and to my family, Allan, Jesse, and David. To Allan, especially, for his support and his art of seeing. Thanks to Maureen Scott Harris and Kitty Lewis, Brick's dazzling women of letters and organization. Heartfelt thanks to Barry Dempster and Daphne Marlatt; and to Don McKay, editor, friend, and compassionate trickster whose wit, keen reading, and virtuosity not only realigned and sharpened these poems, but taught me, and still do.

Biography

Lorri Neilsen Glenn was born and raised in
Western Canada and moved to Nova Scotia in
1983. An ethnographer and essayist, she is the
author and editor of six scholarly books on
research and literacy. She was appointed Poet
Laureate for Halifax for 2005-2009. *Combustion*
is her second book of poetry.